PACIFIC NORTHWEST

Yellow Point Lodge, British Columbia.

COUNTRY INNS OF AMERICA

Pacific Northwest

A GUIDE TO THE INNS OF
OREGON, WASHINGTON, AND BRITISH COLUMBIA

BY FRED T. BUSK, PETER ANDREWS,
AND ROSEMARY ROCHESTER

PHOTOGRAPHED BY FRED T. BUSK AND LILO RAYMOND

DESIGNED BY ROBERT REID

HOLT, RINEHART AND WINSTON, *New York*

AN OWL BOOK

Front cover. Wigwam Inn, British Columbia.
Back cover. Hotel De Haro's restaurant and bar, in a separate house overlooking the dock.

The inns photographed by Lilo Raymond are Salishan Lodge, Timberline Lodge, James House and The Captain Whidbey. All other inns are photographed by Fred Busk. Included are some photographs by his assistant, Margot Rochester. Her photographs appear on pages 10, 19, 22, 31, 52, 60, 66, 68, 69.

Maps prepared by Anthony St. Aubyn.
Editorial assistance by Alan Harvey.

Photographs on the following pages are used with permission from The Knapp Press, 5900 Wilshire Blvd., LA 90036, © 1978 by Knapp Communications Corporation: 24–29, 32–37, 44–49, 56–59.

Copyright © 1981 by Holt, Rinehart and Winston
All rights reserved, including the right to reproduce
this book or portions thereof in any form.
Published by Holt, Rinehart and Winston,
383 Madison Avenue, New York, New York 10017.
Published simultaneously in Canada by Holt, Rinehart
and Winston of Canada, Limited.

Library of Congress Cataloging in Publication Data
Busk, Fred.
    Pacific Northwest, a guide to the inns of
Oregon, Washington, and British Columbia.
    (Country inns of America)
    "An Owl book."
    1.   Hotels, taverns, etc.—Northwest, Pacific—
Directories.   I.   Andrews, Peter, 1931–
II.   Rochester, Rosemary.   III.   Raymond, Lilo.
IV.   Title.   V.   Series.
TX907.B88   647'.9479501   81-1617
ISBN 0-03-059181-3 (pbk.)   AACR2

10 9 8 7 6 5 4 3 2

A Robert Reid - Wieser & Wieser Production

Printed in the United States of America

THE INNS

PACIFIC NORTHWEST

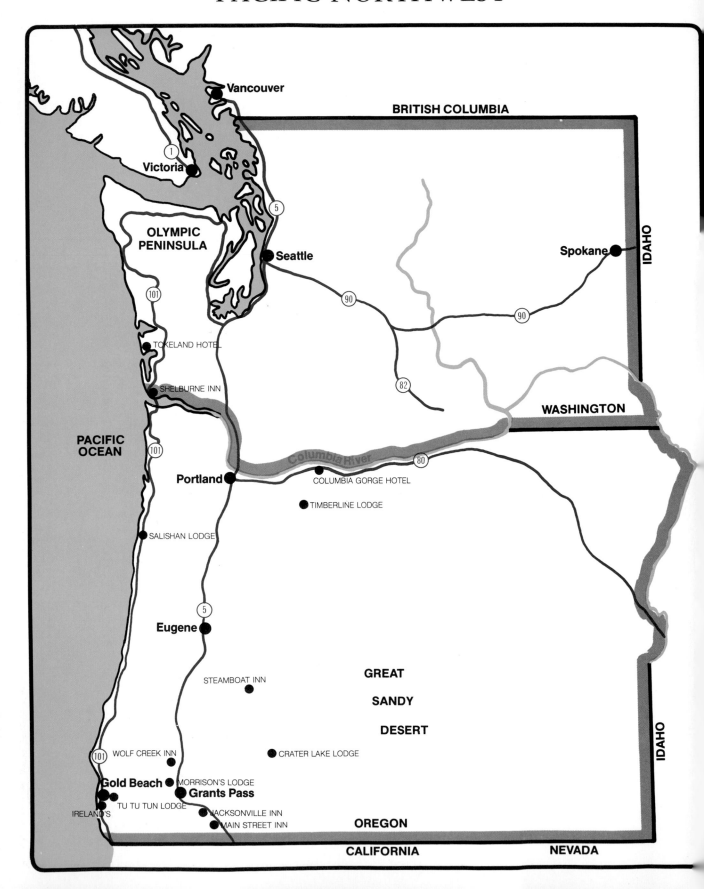

THE SAN JUAN AND GULF ISLANDS

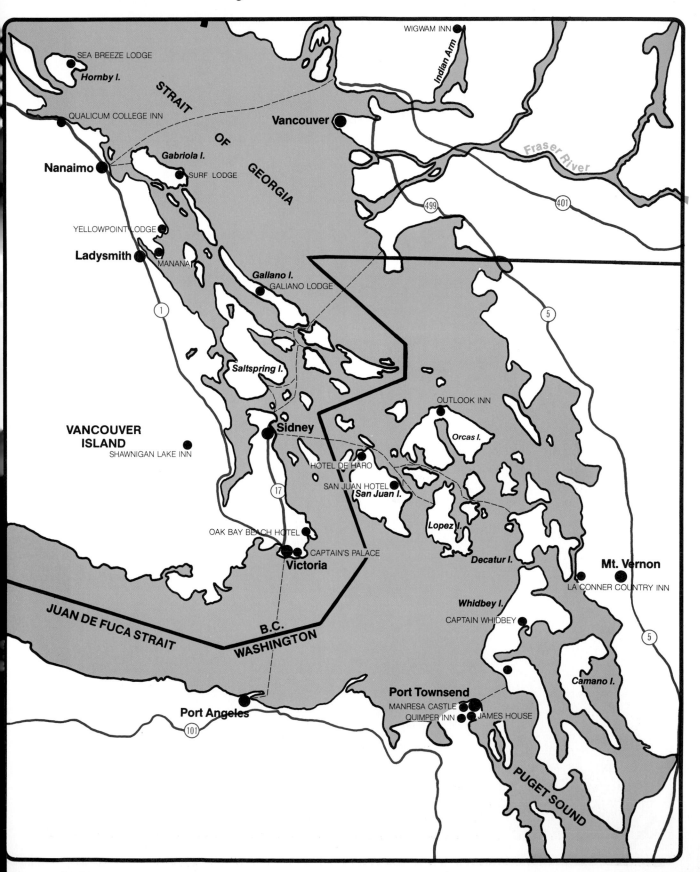

WIGWAM INN

Indian Arm

SEA BREEZE LODGE

Hornby I.

STRAIT

Vancouver

Fraser River

QUALICUM COLLEGE INN

OF

Gabriola I.

Nanaimo

SURF LODGE

GEORGIA

499

401

YELLOWPOINT LODGE

Ladysmith

MANANA

Galiano I.

GALIANO LODGE

1

5

Saltspring I.

OUTLOOK INN

**VANCOUVER
ISLAND**

Sidney

Orcas I.

SHAWNIGAN LAKE INN

HOTEL DE HARO

SAN JUAN HOTEL

San Juan I.

17

Lopez I.

OAK BAY BEACH HOTEL

Decatur I.

Mt. Vernon

CAPTAIN'S PALACE

LA CONNER COUNTRY INN

Victoria

Whidbey I.

CAPTAIN WHIDBEY

JUAN DE FUCA STRAIT

B.C.

5

WASHINGTON

Camano I.

Port Townsend

MANRESA CASTLE

Port Angeles

QUIMPER INN

JAMES HOUSE

101

PUGET SOUND

EDITOR'S NOTE

There are 31 inns described and illustrated in this book. Our photographer and writer visited them all and selected them as outstanding for various reasons: historical interest, food, ambience, innkeepers, furnishings, local amenities. Each inn offers a different mix of characteristics, so study them carefully to determine which ones you might most enjoy. All inngoers have strong personal preferences, and there are inns represented here to suit all tastes.

We have omitted most of the government park lodges that one finds in the Pacific Northwest. They provide a very useful service and are certainly "country inns," though not the kind of personal hostelry we were looking for. The two in Oregon were included for special reasons: Timberline because it is being restored gradually and Crater Lake because of the scenery. There is another special type of inn in the west—the large condominium resort—and we have included the best example, Salishan Lodge.

Visiting a country inn for the first time requires a certain spirit of adventure. Usually an inn is far nicer than we can describe it, but it is also possible for changes to occur—chefs come and go, staffs change—but generally these are temporary, and a visit is usually worthwhile at any time. If not, let us know. And if we have omitted some personal favorites, again let us know so that we can look at them for future editions.

A British Columbia car ferry rounds the lighthouse off Gabriola Island.

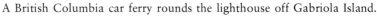

FERRY INFORMATION

Ferries are the major link between the mainland of Washington and British Columbia and the islands in Puget Sound and the Strait of Georgia. The San Juan Islands are a particularly popular year-round recreation area, with many inns and resorts, and it is essential for the traveler to know the departure and arrival points en route to a destination.

Before planning an itinerary, travelers should phone the numbers listed below for specific schedules and rates, which are frequently subject to change. The information provided here is a general guide to the principal ferry terminals and the major stops between them.

Though not carrying cars, the BRITISH COLUMBIA STEAMSHIP CO. runs a passenger service between Seattle, Wash., and Victoria, B.C., through late fall. For information on sailing times, fares, and reservations, phone (800) 623-5560 (Seattle). BLACK BALL TRANSPORT, INC., runs a car ferry from Port Angeles, Wash., to Victoria, B.C. For information, phone (800) 622-2222 (Seattle), or (800) 457-4491 (Port Angeles).

WASHINGTON STATE FERRIES

Car ferries leave Seattle for Bremerton and the Olympic Peninsula; from there you can take U.S.-101 to Port Angeles, or turn off 101 onto Rte. 20 and drive to Port Townsend, where a ferry connects with Keystone on Whidbey Island. There is also a ferry from Seattle to Winslow on Bainbridge Island, and, north of Seattle, there is ferry service from Mukilteo to Clinton on Whidbey Island. Mukilteo is on Rte. 526, west of I-5 and just south of Everett.

Washington State Ferries also serve the San Juan Islands from Anacortes, which is reached via I-5 north to Rte. 20, then west on 20 to the turnoff for Anacortes. Car ferries depart Anacortes for Lopez, Shaw, Orcas, Friday Harbor (San Juan Island), and Sidney, B.C.

For information on Washington State Ferries, phone (800) 464-6400 (Seattle); or (800) 542-0810; (800) 542-7052 (out of area).

BRITISH COLUMBIA FERRIES

Principal terminals of the British Columbia Ferry Corp. are at Tsawwassen on the mainland 20 miles south of Vancouver, and Swartz Bay on Vancouver Island 20 miles north of Victoria. To get to Tsawwassen, take Hwy. 90 south to Hwy. 17, then turn

west to terminal. (From U.S. points, take I-5 north to Hwy. 17.) To get to Swartz Bay, drive to the northern limits of Victoria via Blanchard (Hwy. 17) to terminal.

Other terminals are at Departure Bay, 3 miles north of Nanaimo on Vancouver Island. Take Hwy. 1 to terminal. This connects with Horseshoe Bay on the mainland 13 miles north of Vancouver. Take Hwy. 99 to West Vancouver, then turn north on Upper Levels (99-1) to terminal signs.

There is also service between Brentwood and Mill Bay. Brentwood Bay is between Swartz Bay and Victoria just off Hwy. 17.

From the mainland, there is service between Tsawwassen and Sturdies Bay and Galiano Island. From Vancouver Island, there is service between Swartz Bay and Galiano Island.

For Hornby Island, take Hwy. 19 north from Nanaimo 50 miles to Buckley Bay. Take ferry to Denman Island, then drive across Denman to ferry for Hornby.

For information on all British Columbia Ferry Corp. services, phone (604) 669-1211 (Vancouver) or (604) 386-3431 (Victoria).

Victorian elegance in a town devoted to Shakespeare

Old-fashioned comfort.

Every seasoned traveler must occasionally have mused: Wouldn't it be nice, just for once, to have an unhurried meal, go to a play, and then return to an elegant, old-fashioned guest room for a glass of sherry, a good book, and bed.

Do not despair! There *is* such a place in southwestern Oregon, not far from the California border. The inn is unabashedly feminine in decor and is situated in the hometown of the famous Oregon Shakespearean Festival, one of the oldest such festivals in the country. Both classic and modern plays are presented in two indoor theaters and on an outdoor Elizabethan stage.

When a local ordinance prohibiting overnight accommodations in residential zones was repealed in 1976, Roanne Lyall saw the ideal way to put her mother's lovely Victorian house to use. Empty for three years, it was a veritable white elephant, but neither Roanne nor her mother could bear to part with it.

The possibility of turning the house into an elegant bed-and-breakfast inn soon became a reality. New wiring and plumbing were installed, antique shops and estate auctions were combed for furnishings, and the result is perfection of a sort rarely found in even the most expensive inns.

Each of the three guest rooms is different, but all are spectacular: full of frills, lace, and light. Fresh flowers grace the tables, full-length curtains drape the windows, and a crystal decanter set on each bureau invites guests to fill it with a wine of their choice. Each room has a television set, artfully hidden, so as not to introduce a discordant note into the carefully planned decor.

One room, with twin beds and a cot, is decorated in red and cream. Another, very frilly room is appointed in white and blue with a white-quilted double bed. The third, more masculine in its color scheme of brown and gold, has a double bed with ruffled coverlet, and ruffles likewise trim the bedside tablecloths that hang to the floor.

Faced with such luxury and such comfort, a guest might well recall the words of Romeo: "O blessed, blessed night! I am afeared, being in night, all this is but a dream, too flattering-sweet to be substantial."

Left and above. A genuine Victorian color scheme is an integral part of the restoration of the old mansion. OVERLEAF. Two of the delightful guest rooms illustrate the carefully planned decor of the inn.

ASHLAND'S MAIN STREET INN, 142 No. Main St., Ashland, Ore. 97520; (503) 488-0969; Mrs. Roanne Lyall, Innkeeper. Elegant guest house in Shakespearean Festival town. Open all year. Three guest rooms, $35 to $40, single or double. Includes breakfast Feb. through Oct. only. Children not encouraged; no pets. No credit cards. Sun deck available to guests. Tennis courts in town. Shakespearean theater. Restaurants in town. Skiing at Mt. Ashland.

DIRECTIONS: From north or south, take I-5 to Ashland.

Epicurean dining in a Gold Rush town

The candlelit basement restaurant is totally professional in its operation.

If possible, arrive in Jacksonville early in the morning; early enough for the town to be free of cars and the sun just high enough to illuminate the faded advertisements peeling from the sides of the false-fronted brick buildings. A stray dog sidles by. A man in a white apron bends over to mop the tavern's entrance. Curtains blow out from open second-story windows. The scene conjures up a movie set in the Gold Rush days.

After twenty years in food merchandising, innkeeper Jerry Evans realized his dream of opening a restaurant that would "create for you an epicurean experience in superb dining. A distinctive cuisine, prepared by master chefs." The Jacksonville Inn has become this, and more. In addition to the dining room eight guest rooms with air conditioning and private baths are decorated with "authentic" Western antiques and offer a view of the main street of this restored Gold Rush town, now a National Historic Landmark.

Jerry's merchandising expertise is immediately evident on entering the lobby. It doubles as a wine store, and a very good one, with selections of the choicest wines from California, the Northwest, and Europe. But his real love is the restaurant in the basement, where a "formal yet leisurely style of service . . . has

been instituted so that the delectable food may be savored to the fullest." Tables against the sandstone walls are lit by pinpoint spots; those in the middle by candles. On each table is a single rose, adding a graceful touch to an atmosphere both elegant and intimate. The adjoining bar-lounge has comfortable railroad benches and candlelit tables.

The table d'hôte dinner offers many courses: salad and marinated beans, vegetables, rice or baked potato, soup de jour, pasta, entrée, dessert, and complimentary wine. À la carte meals include salad, rice or potato, and vegetable. The selection is comprehensive: five different cuts of steak, prime ribs, veal, chicken, pork chops, and an excellent selection of fresh seafood. If your tastes run beyond the dining room's comprehensive wine list, Jerry will gladly enlarge the choice to include the more than 400 vintages offered in the lobby store.

This highly professional restaurant located in an unlikely spot is much sought out by visiting connoisseurs of fine food.

All guest rooms have private baths.

Left. The inn is part of a restoration project for the whole street.

JACKSONVILLE INN, 175 E. California St., Jacksonville, Ore. 97530; (503) 899-1900; Jerry and Linda Evans, Innkeepers. Restored hotel and restaurant in picturesque Gold Rush town. Open all year. Eight air-conditioned rooms with private baths. Rates $25 single; $28 to $35 double. Morning coffee by request. Wine and gift shop in hotel lobby. Superlative restaurant and bar lounge in basement. Extensive wine list. Closed Christmas Day and New Year's Eve. Children welcome; small pets allowed. MasterCard, Visa, and American Express credit cards accepted. Entire town National Historic Landmark. Tennis courts; music festival in Aug.; Shakespearean Festival 15 miles from inn in Ashland; 40 miles from ski area.

DIRECTIONS: From Eugene, take I-5 south to Medford. Go east 7 miles on Rte. 238 to Jacksonville.

WOLF CREEK TAVERN

Wolf Creek OREGON

An authentic stagecoach inn on the Oregon Trail

"Travelers avoid risk of ocean travel. . . . Overland mail route to Oregon. Through in six days to Portland!!" With these assurances, the Oregon Stage Line hoped to lure passengers to the overland mail route from California to Portland. The year was 1866 and the Wolf Creek Tavern had been in business for a decade.

So goes one of the colorful, but unauthenticated, stories surrounding the tavern. Others maintain that it was built by a railroad and stagecoach baron; or by Chinese laborers over the tailings of an old gold mine; or that the original structure burned and the existing building was erected on the site. But what *is* certain is that it stands as an imposing relic from the stagecoach era, unique for remaining in almost continuous operation as an inn. A perfect example of nineteenth-century Classical Revival architecture, it is representative of stagecoach inns and hostelries on the early roads of Oregon.

A number of famous guests have reportedly stayed at the tavern: President Rutherford B. Hayes, Jack London (whose wife finished typing one of his manuscripts there), Sinclair Lewis, and movie stars Mary Pickford and Clark Gable.

All the guest rooms have been completely refurnished in various period styles.

In 1975 the Oregon State Park and Recreation Division acquired the tavern. Age and deterioration had taken its toll, but restoration was begun in 1977 and the tavern reopened in 1979. The careful restoration reflects the various periods of the inn's history; the furnishings, some authentic antiques, are a collection of old and new. While the rooms enjoy the contemporary amenities of air conditioning and heat and all guest rooms have private baths, the atmosphere is a faithful rendering of the tavern's various alterations.

Much of the charm and warmth of a bygone era is due to innkeepers Vernon and Donna Wiard, who lease the tavern from the state and run it very well. The food, from hamburgers to more elegant fare, is well prepared and reasonably priced. And for relaxation, it is pleasant to sit in the front parlor next to the fireplace and play a game on the antique checkers table. Unfortunately, the rare square baby grand in the "ladies" parlor does not work; the music would fit right in.

WOLF CREEK TAVERN, Box 97, Wolf Creek, Ore. 97497; (503) 866-2474; Vernon and Donna Wiard, Innkeepers. Cozy, with great atmosphere, this is an authentic restoration of a typical Oregon roadside inn from the heyday of stagecoach travel. Open all year. Eight guest rooms with private baths. Rates per person $19 to $26 single; $23 to $29 double. Dining room seating 38 open to public for 3 meals daily. Children not encouraged; no pets. No credit cards. Fishing for steelhead and salmon is a popular sport and panning for gold is exciting. There is biking on a wilderness trail and rafting in nearby Rogue River.

DIRECTIONS: From Medford, take U.S.-5 north through Grants Pass. Approximately 19 miles north of Grants Pass, take Exit 76 to Wolf Creek. From Portland, take U.S.-5 south to Wolf Creek exit.

Left. The "Ladies' Parlor," as it was called in the old days.

For a fisherman's holiday or a family vacation

This luxurious riverside lodge will appeal to people who take rivers seriously. When a 1964 flood swept their cabins away, innkeepers Elaine and B. A. Hanten rebuilt comfortable duplexes raised on posts.

Every conceivable river activity is available at Morrison's. There are daily jet-boat trips and three- and four-day rafting trips. The Rogue River is famous for fishing and is one of the reasons sportsmen return year after year. The second is the food—good, old-fashioned, and abundant, served family style in the spacious dining room. Canadian bacon soup, prime ribs and Yorkshire pudding, broccoli soufflé, wild berry pies, and sourdough pancakes are a few highlights.

The lodge living room with wide windows, stone fireplace flanked by big comfortable armchairs and grand piano, is a relaxing gathering place for guests who do not have their own air-conditioned housekeeping cottages with fireplaces.

MORRISON'S LODGE, 8500 Galice Rd., Merlin, Ore. 97532; (503) 476-3825; Elaine and B. A. Hanten, Innkeepers. Originally built as a fall and winter steelhead fishing lodge, Morrison's has been expanded to provide an attractive variety of activities for a family vacation. Open May 1 to Nov. 15. Sept. 15 to Nov. 15, $75 per person, per day, with 3 superb meals. Off season (June, July, Aug. only), dinner, lodging and breakfast, $40 per person. Housekeeping cottages, per day (2-day minimum stay) 2 persons $60, 3 persons $90, 4 persons $100. Overnight stay $32 per person, double occupancy. Dining room open to inn guests only. Lunch baskets available for boaters and rafters. Children welcome; no pets. No credit cards. Fishing, swimming (river and pool), floating (rubber raft, inner tube, or air mattress), tennis, putting green, hiking, gold panning, rock hounding, visits to Oregon Caves, Crater Lake, the Pacific Ocean, and Shakespearean Festival in Ashland. Write for raft and boating trip rates.

DIRECTIONS: Transportation to and from Grants Pass airport and bus terminal, no charge. Driving from Grants Pass, take U.S.-5 north to Merlin exit (Galice Rd.). Inn is 12 miles.

Gold Beach IRELAND'S RUSTIC LODGES

The ocean blue and the wilderness too

Since the early 1930s, this modestly priced inn has been welcoming guests to Oregon's magnificent south coast. Ideally situated between the highway and the sea, Ireland's cabins are surrounded by beautiful gardens beneath towering pines. Guest rooms in the lodge have ocean views, and all rooms and cabins have handsome stone fireplaces, color TV, and private baths.

The inn has no restaurant, but the Captain's Table, a half block away, serves inexpensive meals and specializes in excellent fish dishes.

The beach below the inn is a favorite hunting ground for agates and driftwood, while the nearby Rogue River is a world-famous fishing ground. Ireland's is a fine stopping place for those who wish to try their skill on this noted waterway. And nature buffs will enjoy the 64- and 104-mile jet-boat rides upriver through an unspoiled wilderness.

IRELAND'S RUSTIC LODGES, Box 774, Gold Beach, Ore. 97444; (503) 247-7718; Mr. and Mrs. Rolf Richmond, Owners; Mr. and Mrs. Billy Routh, Managers. Superior motel-type accommodations in handsome rustic cabins or main lodge overlooking ocean. Open all year. Double occupancy rates, cabins $25 to $36; lodge rooms $36. Each additional person in room $5. Children welcome; no pets. No credit cards. No restaurant, but Captain's Table nearby serves 3 meals daily. Beachcombing, fishing, horseback riding, jet-boat rides.

DIRECTIONS: From California and southern points, take U.S.-101 north to Gold Beach. From northern Oregon, take U.S.-101 south.

Gold Beach # TU TU TUN LODGE **OREGON**

The guest lodge, with luxury modern interiors.

Fisherman's paradise on the famed Rogue River

Seven miles from Oregon's spectacular scenic coast, this contemporary rustic lodge is situated on the banks of the famed Rogue River. Fishing is the lodge's raison d'être. Chinook salmon run the river in spring and again in fall; offshore ocean fishing is at its best during July and August; the Rogue's famous steelhead runs are from late August through October. Jet boats skim the shallow riffles and most turbulent spots to transport guests to the hottest fishing grounds. Nonfishermen will find ample recreation on the grounds or nearby. Upriver excursion boats stop at the lodge's dock to take guests on scenic cruises. The river teems with wildlife, and lucky guests might spot bear, deer, otter, beaver, heron, and osprey.

Ralph Priestley, an architect, designed, built, and ran the lodge with his wife until daughter and son-in-law Laurie and Dirk Van Zante took over in 1979. The main building is constructed around a massive central fireplace about ten paces from the bar, where guests flock after a day's fishing. Low, comfortable tables fill the space between. Dinner is served family style at large round tables, a relaxed atmosphere in which to enjoy the unsurpassed menu of meats, seafood, guests' fresh-caught fish, vegetables, fruits, and desserts. Early rising fishermen will find their breakfast favorites awaiting them and if requested a hearty lunch will be packed for the trip.

Guest accommodations are in a separate, two-story building. Each room opens through a sliding glass door onto a balcony overlooking the river and swimming pool. The contemporary and comfortable rooms, each with private bath, are equipped with racks for fishing rods and outdoor gear.

When night falls, fires are lit in outside fireplaces, and guests move to the terrace for talk about the day's activities or to just listen to the sounds of river and forest.

Exclusivity exacts a price, but this fisherman's paradise and vacationer's hideaway is well worth the cost. It combines all the charm of a rustic lodge with the comforts and conveniences of a modern resort.

The main lodge interior is Northwest rustic modern at its best.

Left. The sparkling pool, main lodge, and happy guests.

TU TU TUN LODGE, North Bank Rd., Rte. 1, Box 365, Gold Beach, Ore. 97444; (503) 247-6664; Laurie and Dirk Van Zante, Innkeepers. Exclusive wilderness vacation and fishing lodge. Open May 1 to Nov. 1. Accommodations for 40 guests. River-view rooms, private bath and balcony $50 single; $57 double. One or 2 additional persons in room, $6 each. Rates do not include meals. Dining room, open to public by reservation only, serves 3 meals a day; lunch baskets available for boaters and fishermen. Children welcome; pets $3 a night. MasterCard and Visa credit cards accepted. Fishing, jet-boat trips, horseback riding, heated swimming pool, horseshoes, 4-hole pitch and putt golf course. Guides provided for fishing.

DIRECTIONS: From California and southern points, take U.S.-101 north to north end of Rogue River Bridge at Gold Beach; turn up river 7 miles to lodge. From northern Oregon, take U.S.-101 south.

CRATER LAKE LODGE

A jewel of a lake in the wilderness

This spectacular lake was created more than 6,000 years ago when a volcanic eruption destroyed a mountain, leaving a crater now filled with water almost 2,000 feet deep. The principal attraction of Crater Lake National Park, it is one of the great natural wonders of America. The wood and stone lodge was artfully designed to blend with the surroundings. It is rustic, but with a certain grandeur. The huge stone fireplace in the lobby sheds warmth; the massive beams in the lounge and dining room provide solidity. Comfortable rooms in the lodge, cabins convenient for families, and good hearty food make Crater Lake Lodge a secure haven in the midst of an awesome and formidable wilderness.

CRATER LAKE LODGE, Crater Lake, Ore. 97604; (503) 594-2511; George Happle, General Manager. Open June 15 to Sept. 10. Rates, with bath, double and single $37. Twin with bath, single and double $35 to $44. Cabins $35 to $45. Lower rates for rooms with shared baths. Cafeteria serves 3 meals a day; breakfast and dinner in dining room; cocktail lounge. Children welcome; pets allowed in cabins. No fishing, but lake boat trips; many hiking trails.

DIRECTIONS: From California and points south, take I-5 to Medford, Ore. Go north on Rte. 62 to Crater Lake National Park. From the north, take I-5 south to Medford.

Idleyld Park

STEAMBOAT INN

OREGON

A rustic, riverside inn that serves a fabulous dinner

Steamboat Inn is a vacation spot that longtime guests like to keep secret. Even your best friends will not tell you! This rustic inn traces its beginnings to early North Umpqua River fishing camps. From the early 1930s until 1954, the lodge was across the river. In 1957 the owners started to build cabins, and since 1975 current innkeepers Jim and Sharon Van Loan have continued the place's colorful traditions. The inn is famous for its fisherman's dinner, a multi-course extravaganza served on a huge table that dominates the dining room. It is available nightly during the summer and on weekends in winter. Guests drive miles for this meal, and reservations are essential. The overnight guest rooms are located in simple but beautiful cabins overlooking the river. The inn's hospitable motto is: "You are a stranger here but once."

STEAMBOAT INN, Toketee Rte., Box 36, Idleyld Park, Ore. 97447; (503) 496-3495 or (503) 498-2411; Jim and Sharon Van Loan, Innkeepers. A beautiful wilderness lodge on the North Umpqua River. Fresh flowers are abundant and the main lodge has a welcoming fireplace. The inn hides its beauties from the highway, but in back, where the cabins are, it is truly gorgeous. Open all year. Six rustic cabins with bath and shower, each $32 for couple or family, not including meals. Dining room, serving 3 meals a day, open to the public by reservation. Special fisherman's dinner served nightly in summer; weekends in winter. Children welcome; pets at innkeepers' discretion (check in advance of stay). No credit cards. Probably most popular recreation is enjoying the great food. There is also swimming, fishing, and hiking the many wilderness trails. Umpqua National Forest, Lookout Mountain nearby.

DIRECTIONS: From Eugene, Ore., take U.S.-5 south to Rte. 138 at Roseburg. Continue east on Rte. 138 to Idleyld Park.

The wild Oregon coast in a luxurious setting

The coastline of northern Oregon is an area of awesome natural beauty, with unspoiled beaches and high capes thrusting out into the ocean. Huge offshore rocks are whipped by winds and spray. The whole strand has a timeless, primeval quality. The surprise is not that this particular stretch of coastline has become the family playground of Oregon, but that the area was developed with such a meticulous eye for the delicate balance of nature.

Salishan Lodge, a modern resort hotel with golf courses, tennis courts, and facilities for small conventions, has been constructed with loving care for the environment. The lodge's 150 guest accommodations are all attached to the main building by covered walkways, but guests have the feeling of being tucked away in a setting of natural wilderness. All guest rooms have handsome brick fireplaces and mammoth baths. Constructed from native Douglas fir and cedar, they are rugged rooms; yet they have touches of luxury and elegance, including contemporary artworks by Oregon artists.

The interiors of the public rooms are studies in contrasts, combining light and dark, intimacy and grandeur. The Gourmet Dining Room has an international reputation. Built on three levels, it has windows everywhere to let diners enjoy the view of Siletz Bay and the ocean beyond.

Salishan is famous for its salmon barbecues where the chef prepares whole, standing sides of salmon on an open charcoal grate. Seafood is a daily specialty from filet of sole Marguery, with tiny shrimp in a delicate cream sauce, to the delicious *coulibiac,* a filet of Chinook salmon layered with mushrooms, rice, onion, and shrimp and baked in a puff pastry. The menu also offers a full range of international dishes.

Recreation at Salishan is built around enjoyment of the outdoors. Facilities for major outdoor sports are available, but many guests do not bother with organized activities; just walking around the area is enough to satisfy. The lodge is part of an 800-acre preserve with trails throughout. A printed botanical

Part of the main lodge, showing the oriental influences in the landscaping.

guide gives detailed descriptions of the 45 different species of local plants. Salishan is also a favorite spot for bird-watchers, and the lodge employs a knowledgeable guide to lead children on nature walks.

Salishan Lodge demonstrates that it is possible to live close to nature in a splendid setting and yet forfeit none of the joys of civilization.

SALISHAN LODGE, Box 118, Gleneden Beach, Ore. 97388; (503) 764-2371; Russ Cleveland, General Manager. A luxurious 150-room resort on the coast of northern Oregon. Open all year. Rates $50 to $94, double occupancy. All rooms have private bath, fireplace, balcony, color TV. Elegant Gourmet Room, serving continental and American cuisine, open to public for 3 meals a day; Sun Room coffee shop for casual dining. Children welcome; pets $4 a day. MasterCard, Visa, and American Express credit cards accepted. Indoor tennis courts, swimming pool, 18-hole golf course, gymnasiums, sauna, whirlpool, billiard room, children's playground, beauty salon.

DIRECTIONS: On U.S.-101, 20 miles north of Newport and just south of Lincoln City. Siletz Bay State Airport ½ mile from lodge. Pickup service.

Left. The Gourmet Dining Room, enclosed by a sweeping panorama of water and greenery. OVERLEAF. The comfortable lounge in the main lodge and, right, one of the guest lodges designed by architect John Storrs. The following spread shows the Oregon coast with its bleached driftwood coveted by sculptors.

PHOTOGRAPHED BY LILO RAYMOND

Hood River COLUMBIA GORGE HOTEL OREGON

The hotel is restored, the view is untouched

"A house of refinement situated in one of the nation's most beautiful sectors. . . . A rushing mountain stream bisecting the park constitutes a million-dollar front yard. Wah-Gwin-Gwin Falls tumbling two hundred and seven feet into the famous Columbia Gorge forms a billion-dollar back yard."

This modest advertisement, written in 1921, is still an accurate description of this eclectic hotel. From the road it resembles a California mansion with a bit of Spanish influence. From the river it appears a castle, with sturdy stone walls clinging to the cliff's edge. On the grounds there is a suggestion of the East in gently arched bridges spanning the stream and Oriental lamps lighting paths to the falls at the hotel's back door. Guests view the falls by leaning over the reassuringly thick stone wall or by bravely edging out onto a viewing platform that seems to overhang the drop.

To visit the hotel is to revisit the 1920s, when lumber millionaire Simon Benson, who had supported construction of the Columbia Gorge Scenic Highway, spent over half a million dollars to build a dream—the Columbia Gorge Hotel. Completely restored to its original opulence, the hotel boasts that every guest room captures that unforgettable era and that no two rooms are alike. Some have cozy fireplaces, others elaborate, king-sized canopied beds; but all share the beauty of gleaming mahogany and brass. And the amenities that today are essentially forgotten are still observed here—oversized bath towels, the morning paper at your door.

The dining room is vast, a small sea of white linen, silverware, and high-backed Queen Anne chairs. And the food matches the decor. From the outset, the hotel has been famous for its cuisine, and it continues the tradition. Columbia River salmon is still a favorite specialty, along with Hood River apple pie. Service is professional and courteous, and portions tempt one to overindulgence. Breakfast offers substantial selections, and on weekends a bountiful country-style breakfast is served.

Located in an area offering many recreational activities, the Columbia Gorge is a hotel the visitor will leave reluctantly.

The restored lobby.

Left. The drive up the Columbia river from Portland is magnificent. This is the view from the hotel.

COLUMBIA GORGE HOTEL, 400 West Cliff Dr., Hood River, Ore. 97031; (503) 386-5566; Mrs. Jackie Muncey, Manager. Palatial 1920s-style hotel on spectacular site. Open all year. Twenty-three guest rooms; private and shared baths. $34 single; $42 to $90 double. Dining room seating 148, open to public for 3 meals a day. Children, pets, welcome. MasterCard, Visa, American Express credit cards accepted. Golf and swimming nearby; boating on river; near Mt. Hood ski area.

DIRECTIONS: From Portland, take I-80 north to Hood River.

Government Camp # TIMBERLINE LODGE

A tribute to man's perseverance

This magnificent ski lodge, 6,000 feet up Mount Hood, was built during the great Depression. Hundreds of unemployed men were put to work on the project by the Works Progress Administration and the Civilian Conservation Corps.

European stonemasons were brought in to teach the Americans the craft. Volcanic stones from nearby canyons were chiseled into shape to build the central fireplace with its chimney nearly 100 feet high. The huge Ponderosa pine pillars that support the roof of the central space were cut in nearby forests. Working with a master blacksmith, the men created a unique collection of handwrought gates, light fixtures, ornaments, and hardware. The sturdy furniture was constructed with strap iron; chair seats were made of laced rawhide; chair backs and table tops were crafted from hardwood planks.

When President Franklin D. Roosevelt dedicated the lodge, he called it "a monument to the skill and faithful performance of workers." Today guests can only marvel at how much beauty was created by relatively unskilled labor. The lobby is the size of a small cathedral. On the staircases the newel posts are made from cedar utility poles and topped with a carved sculpture of a native bird or animal. At the head of the front staircase, a huge door opens onto a balcony, offering a sweeping view of Mount Hood's forested slopes and the valley far below.

Although the lodge operates year-round, it is at its most spectacular when buried in snow and ice, especially as shown OVERLEAF.

The guest rooms are furnished with pieces especially designed for the lodge and reflect the Art Deco style in vogue in the 1930s. Although the furniture is massive and very sturdy, Richard L. Kohnstamm, the area operator, was concerned that in time with the inn's constant traffic the designs for the rugs, draperies, and bedspreads would be lost. He and other Oregonians organized Friends of Timberline, a group that is restoring many rooms to their original state and has made new appliquéd draperies and spreads and hooked new rugs, all according to the original designs.

The lodge has fifty guest rooms with private baths. The restaurant serves three meals daily and the Ram's Head Bar is a comfortable place to relax after a day of skiing. In addition there is swimming in the lodge pool, to unwind after a day on the slopes or to relax in preparation for an evening around the fire.

Left. A balustrade of sawed-off telephone poles borders the Ram's Head Bar and forms a balcony around the lobby, where the grandiose chimney soars up through the roof, *above*. OVERLEAF. The photographs following the lodge show a ski class in progress and, right, the Blue Gentian Room, recently restored to the original designs of the 1930s.

TIMBERLINE LODGE, Government Camp, Ore. 97028; (503) 231-5400; Richard L. Kohnstamm, Area Operator; Dawson Hubert, General Manager. America's first year-round ski resort. Fifty-room lodge offers a variety of accommodations from $26 single; $26 to $75 double. Private baths except in bunk rooms. Write for descriptive brochure for accommodations, winter lift rates, ski lessons, package plans, and special events. Restaurants, open to public, include Cascade Dining Room, featuring continental cuisine; cafeteria-style Ski Deli; and snack bar. Children welcome; supervised playroom for ages 2 to 8. No pets. MasterCard, Visa, and American Express credit cards accepted. Gift shop, ski shop, heated swimming pool, downhill and cross-country skiing. Tourist chair lift rides in summer.

DIRECTIONS: From Portland, take U.S.-26 to Government Camp. Trailways Bus service from Portland; Timberline shuttle.

PHOTOGRAPHED BY LILO RAYMOND

SHELBURNE INN

Seaview WASHINGTON

Sleep in a real antique bed—before it's sold out from under you

One hundred years ago, wealthy Portlanders considered the Shelburne "*the* place to go." But times have changed. The railroad no longer runs to the peninsula and the pace of life is not what it once was.

When David Campiche first saw the famed inn in run-down condition, it saddened his antiquarian's heart. So he bought it, replumbed and rewired it, and with wife Laurie Anderson's help gradually restored it to its present pristine state. The inn is unusual in that it doubles as an antique shop. Since practically everything is for sale, the inn's decor is constantly changing. To reach the registration desk (once a church altar), guests struggle through a collection of oak dressers, pub signs, pianos, clocks, and dry sinks.

The fifteen guest rooms are showpieces of early American comfort. It is not unusual to find people wandering through them wondering aloud how they can duplicate the inn's homeyness in their own houses. For some, it is easy: they just buy their room and take it home! (But not the lace curtains and antique quilts.)

The restaurant is leased to Nanci Main and Jimella Lucas, who had been looking for some time for a place where they could branch out on their own. After years of apprenticing and working as chefs in Portland and Seattle restaurants, they were ready for their own place. They found it at the Shelburne Inn. The restaurant has received accolades from the day it opened. William Rice, executive food editor of *The Washington Post* and co-author of *Where to Eat in America* says: "It's like discovering an excellent restaurant in an out-of-the-way village in France, the kind the world beats a path to once the word gets out."

Nanci is a baking specialist, Jimella the seafood expert; and the menu gives full rein to their talents. On the menu may be halibut Florentine, prawns Provençale, sturgeon Bordelaise, and bouillabaisse, a house specialty, aromatic and rich after thirty hours of carefully attended simmering. The desserts are, as Nanci puts it, "decadent." "We are two people excited about food who will identify with every item

The dining room is the preserve of chefs Nanci Main and Jimella Lucas, a brilliant team producing superb food.

that comes out of the kitchen," says Nanci. Laurie and David agree; so does James Beard, a frequent guest and ardent fan.

Today guests flock from Seattle and Portland, and once again the Shelburne Inn is "*the* place to go."

THE SHELBURNE INN, Box 250; Seaview, Wash. 98644; (206) 642-2442; David Campiche and Laurie Anderson, Innkeepers. Restaurant (206) 642-4142; Nanci Main and Jimella Lucas, Owner-Chefs. The past comes alive in this restored Victorian inn. Open all year. Fifteen antique-filled guest rooms with shared baths. Rates by the room: $24 one double bed, $30 two double beds. Includes continental breakfast. Restaurant has an enviable reputation for fine lunches and dinners. All entrées cooked to order, whether for 5 or 100. Children welcome; no pets. MasterCard and Visa credit cards accepted. Interesting shops in town. Beach. Entire inn is an antique shop with most furnishings for sale. David also runs a shop in nearby Long Beach.

DIRECTIONS: From Aberdeen, take U.S.-101 south to junction with Rte. 103. Go north to Seaview. Inn on left side of Rte. 103 at J St. Watch for large inn sign.

Left. The perfectly restored 100-year-old inn and one of the attractive guest rooms.

Everything is family style at this antiques-filled inn

"People are always bringing us things," says Betty Smith, half hidden by ferns and a wire birdcage. "They bring us old dishes and books and pictures, things they want other people to see and enjoy." As Mrs. Smith talks, some women move around the dining room making new arrangements on the tables from baskets of fresh flowers they have brought from their gardens. They do this twice a week.

A group of guests sitting in white wicker chairs in the plant-filled lobby finishes tea and, bill paid, call Betty aside and tell her how much they enjoyed themselves. One says, "We're all very proud of what Betty is doing, you know."

The Tokeland Hotel restoration is very much a community effort. When, after four years of hard work, a succession of family tragedies threatened Al and Betty Smith's dream, friends came, rolled up their sleeves, and started scraping paint.

The work continues, soon, it is hoped, to be assisted by a grant, now that the hotel has been placed on the state Register of Historic Places.

Left. The portraits are no one in particular—just part of the innkeepers' growing collection of incredible memorabilia. **OVERLEAF.** The dining room and lounge house more collectibles.

One of the restored guest rooms.

The upstairs guest rooms are in various stages of completion, but all are comfortable, bright, and airy. The main floor, the heart of the hotel, is finished and is chock-a-block with collections of plates and objects that seem to overflow onto the candy counter that serves as a registration desk and spill over the two pianos separating the lounge and dining room. Betty is comfortable with the mix of things; somehow she makes it work. She has been collecting antiques since she was six and likes to arrange and display her finds. It is part of the style of the Tokeland.

Charlotte Brown, wife of the first homesteader on Toke Point, is supposed to have said, "When the tide is out, the table is set." It sums up the abundance of fish and game in the area, blessed as it is with a temperate climate. It well describes the food at the Tokeland, food for families, creatively prepared and served by Betty and her staff dressed in period costumes. The reasonably priced dinners all include salad, vegetable, potato, and homemade bread. It is nice to find family style dinners: baked ham, roast beef, baked chicken. It is in keeping with the feeling of the Tokeland, families and friends enjoying being together.

TOKELAND HOTEL, Box 117, Tokeland, Wash. 98590; (206) 267-4700; Betty and Al Smith, Innkeepers. This 1885 farmhouse is now a restaurant and inn noted for good food and the whimsicality of its decor. Open all year. Seventeen guest rooms share 4 baths and 1 shower. All rooms have double beds; rates $25 to $30 per room. Dining room, open to public, serves 3 meals a day except Tuesday and Wednesday in winter. Children not encouraged; no pets. Master-Card, Visa credit cards accepted. Sunbathing on lawn; swimming at adjacent beach.

DIRECTIONS: From Tacoma, take I-5 to Olympia; go west on Rte. 8 to Aberdeen; go south on Rte. 101 to junction of Rte. 105. Turn right, watch for sign. Hotel is on corner of Kindred Ave. and Hotel Rd.

Spectacular views from every elegant room

This substantial mansion, once the home of a wealthy businessman in this former boom town, James House went to seed after his death. In the early 1960s Bill and Frances Eaton set to work on a massive restoration. After nine years, it had regained all its old luster.

The present owners, Lowell and Barbara Bogart, bought the house in 1976. "We slept in it one night," Lowell recalls, "and we owned the place the next day." The Bogarts maintained the Eatons' high standards and added several graceful touches of their own. Barbara keeps a variety of beautiful plants in the two expansively furnished parlors on the main floor and at windows in the guest rooms. The ten guest rooms include garden suites on the ground floor, one with a fireplace, a spool bed, and another bed with a cane headboard.

Upstairs are a number of decorating blockbusters. In one room there is a carved Oriental sofa and two chairs with armrests in the shape of dragons. In another is a brass-banded oak bedroom set with a carved acorn motif. But the most luxurious accommodation is the bridal suite, a full-blown Victorian extravaganza. The bed has a magnificent headboard with panels of walnut burl. In the anteroom is a long red fainting couch, a Victorian rocker, and an armchair placed in the four-window bay with a view of Port Townsend. A single rose is the Bogarts' daily offering in the bridal suite. Couples celebrating a significant event are also likely to find champagne cooling in a silver bucket.

A room with a view at the James House is not to be taken lightly, for all around the town and across the water rise high mountains, snow capped through most of the year.

Breakfast at the James House is served each day in the kitchen, where guests gather around an oak table in front of a big iron cookstove. The Bogarts serve a dozen different kinds of homemade bread. Lowell toasts thick pieces and hands around butter and his

Left. The bridal suite boasts a spacious antechamber with a view of Port Townsend Bay.

A single rose is the Bogarts' daily offering in the bridal suite.

own homemade pear preserves. People linger over coffee, while Barbara makes sure all the guests are introduced to each other.

At Port Townsend one begins not only to understand the great dreams of the first developers but to credit the restorers for their fidelity to what the nineteenth century achieved. Thanks to the high standards of the Eatons and the Bogarts, the James House is once again the finest home in town.

JAMES HOUSE, 1238 Washington St., Port Townsend, Wash. 98368; (206) 385-1238; Lowell and Barbara Bogart, Innkeepers. One of the finest Victorian mansions in this historic town. Open all year. Ten guest rooms, including suites. Private and shared baths. Rates, including continental breakfast, $28 to $32 single; $40 to $56 (suite) double. Children over 12 welcome; no pets. No credit cards. Croquet on inn grounds; tennis, golf, swimming in town. Hiking and sightseeing.

DIRECTIONS: From Seattle, take ferry to Winslow. Follow signs to Hood Canal ferry; after crossing, follow signs to Port Townsend. The James House is in the upper town on the road running along edge of bluff, next to post office.

Left. The inn building has been repainted in shades of light gray, but the beautiful red roof is the same.
This page. A view of the bay from the front porch; a Garland stove in one of the garden suites; the living room, whose original furniture was discovered in the carriage house. OVERLEAF. The ferry leaving Port Townsend for Whidbey Island.

Dark Roast
Decaffeinated
Dark Roast
Colombi
Roast
French Roast
Colman's
MUST
JACOB & Co
Crackers
THE BOOK OF TOFU
Webster's

Port Townsend # QUIMPER INN **WASHINGTON**

A gifted innkeeper brings an art-filled inn alive

The two-story house is not painted in any usual way. A paper carp floats from the second floor porch. A pretty, dark-haired young woman walks through the door balancing two pumpkins and a basket of flowers. These clues might lead one to think the Quimper Inn holds interesting surprises—and it does.

Built as a home in 1880, it has been a boarding house, a warehouse, a ghost house, and then, upon renovation, a bed-and-breakfast inn until 1969, when Marii and Matthew Jacobs bought it. Faced with only minimal renovations, the Jacobses set out to make the Quimper a decorating tour de force.

Each guest room has a theme. The inn's pamphlet describes them: "Rose and Thistle—queen size bed, large bay window, mountain view." "Gaff Schooner —large bay windows, sunrise, bay and mountain views, double bed in one room; adjoining room with bath including antique tin tub. . . ."

Marii's considerable talent as an artist and her attention to detail are evident in the rooms. There are foil-wrapped mints on each pillow, sachets on the dresser, small still-lifes, little vignettes on walls or bedside tables coordinated to the tone of the room. In Marii's distinctive hand are quotes: "Art is not a thing . . . it is a way."—Oscar Wilde. And so it is; there are good books on tables and current magazines in baskets.

This sort of creative pleasure pervades the inn, named Quimper after the first mate of Captain Vancouver's ship *Discovery*. The living room is filled with music, flowers, and early American antiques; books on the arts are everywhere.

A glimpse into the kitchen reveals a sky-blue, enameled wood stove holding bottles of homemade herb vinegars, jams, and jellies. Garlands of onions and garlic hang among shining pots; bowls of fruit glow in the sunlight.

A large harvest table dominates the dining room, where large windows overlook the garden. Today

breakfast is fresh cantaloupe with sliced kiwi fruit garnished with nasturtiums. Freshly made whole-wheat blueberry croissants are served with sweet butter, jam, jellies, honey, marmalade and welcome cups of strong French roast coffee.

The observant guest will notice that during the night the table centerpieces, the flowers, and even the ribbons on the candlesticks have been changed. And if you listen, you might hear Marii chopping wood out back just to keep busy, and because she "likes to exercise."

QUIMPER INN, 1306 Franklin, Port Townsend, Wash. 98368; (206) 385-1086; Matthew and Marii Jacobs Innkeepers. An unusual bed-and-breakfast filled with unexpected artistic touches. Open all year. Six guest rooms, private and shared baths, $35 including breakfast, the only meal served. Children over 10 welcome; no pets; no smoking. No credit cards. Croquet, tennis, golf, swimming in town, bicycling, hiking, sightseeing.

DIRECTIONS: From Seattle, take ferry to Winslow. Follow signs to Hood Canal ferry; after crossing, follow signs to Port Townsend. Inn is on Franklin, between Harrison and Van Buren Sts.

Left. This corner of the kitchen focuses on the fine old preserved wood stove. Every part of the inn demonstrates superb taste and fastidious attention to details, as shown OVERLEAF: a bathroom with its prized zinc tub; a breakfast table setting highlighted by the morning sun; a guest room showing a beautiful old quilt.

Rhenish relic of boom-town prosperity

The wood-paneled lounge is dark, intimate, and hushed; outside the large windows gleam the evening lights of the harbor. Hard to imagine that this inn was once a Jesuit school. It seems more fitting to recall the original owner, Charles Eisenbeis, a Prussian tycoon who made a fortune during the bonanza years of Port Townsend. The town's first mayor, Eisenbeis drew on his memories of castles on the Rhine to build this romantic home as a gift for his young bride.

Located at the junction of the Strait of Juan de Fuca and Puget Sound, Port Townsend seemed a natural seaport. Spurred by dreams of riches to be made in timber, shipping, and the promise of a railhead, early settlers built ornate, solid buildings around the harbor, and the high bluffs above the town soon bristled with elaborate Victorian mansions. The town boomed for ten years; then the bubble burst when the railroad never materialized.

The castle remained empty until it became a Jesuit school, enlarged and named Manresa after the Spanish town where the order was founded. The Jesuits' departure left the building again untenanted.

In 1973 Ron Smith looked at the castle after his wife, Carol, saw it advertised on a supermarket bulletin board. Possibly Ron's background as a consulting computer engineer allowed him to overlook, or come to terms with, the obstacles inherent in renovating the place. But the Smiths have not only done it; they have done it with style. Carol tastefully decorated each of the forty-five guest rooms with antiques. Many afford a wonderful view of the bay and mountains.

There are two dining rooms: an informal one off the foyer, bright with calico flowers and gold tablecloths, and the main dining room adjoining the luxurious lounge.

The menu draws on the abundant local seafood, as well as offering steak and such delicious specialties as curry of prawns and chicken, or steak and oysters. The wine list features local and imported wines. Mouthwatering desserts are presented on a cart rolled to the table.

Guests will enjoy strolling in the formal gardens and studying the castle's old-world carved woodwork. It could be *the* place to stay during Port Townsend's twice yearly open house. After trudging through Victorian homes rich in period antiques and memories, then sitting in the castle lounge with a drink, looking out on the harbor, one may wonder "what would it have been like if the railroad had not gone to Seattle . . .?"

A finely carved sideboard and a German grandfather clock decorate the lobby.

Left. One of the forty-five guest rooms, all furnished with antiques.

MANRESA CASTLE, Box 564, 7th and Sheridan, Port Townsend, Wash. 98368; (206) 385-5750; Ron and Carol Smith, Innkeepers. Large baronial mansion with spectacular views of city, harbor, and mountains. Open all year. Rates for guest rooms and suites $35 to $40, double occupancy. Private baths, TV, and telephones. Continental rooms with family plan, no private bath, 1 bed $26; 2 beds $29. Single persons $10 less; extra guest in room $5. Only full-service restaurant in town serves 3 meals a day; open to public. Children welcome; no charge under 12. Small pets $4. MasterCard and Visa credit cards accepted. Tennis, golf, swimming nearby. Sightseeing; ferry to Whidbey Is.

DIRECTIONS: From Seattle, take ferry to Winslow. Follow signs to Hood Canal ferry; after crossing, follow signs to Port Townsend. Take Rte. 20 (Sims Way) to Sheridan. Watch for signs.

THE CAPTAIN WHIDBEY

Whidbey Island   **WASHINGTON**

A rustic retreat only 90 minutes from Seattle

The local magistrate on Whidbey Island around the turn of the century, Judge Lester Still laid out his plans for a summer resort hotel in 1907 and had it built entirely of madrona logs. Madrona wood is lovely to look at but difficult to work with. But the trees were indigenous and the judge liked them—so madrona it was.

The inn was a success from the start, and summer vacationers sailed over from Tacoma and Seattle to tie up at the judge's dock on Penn Cove. The John C. Stone family took over the inn's ownership in 1964. Today it is very much a family-run establishment, with sons Geoff and John presiding over most of the inn's management.

Rooms at the inn are generally short on space but long on rustic charm. They are furnished with local pieces, and all have handsome marble-topped washstands. The adjoining cottages are somewhat larger with their own sitting rooms and fireplaces. Across the property, on a small inlet off Penn Cove, are the lagoon buildings. These offer spacious rooms with private baths, usually an antique chest or table, and a view of the bucolic shores that surround Whidbey, an island with a heritage not only of seafaring men but of farmers and loggers as well.

Now accessible by both bridge and ferry, the Captain Whidbey is only ninety minutes from Seattle, and its restaurant has become popular the year around. The Chart Room, a lively cocktail lounge, is furnished with a happy jumble of artifacts. The dining room is cheerful with windows along the wall that overlook the cove. Seafood is naturally featured, but four times a year there is a theme dinner party. In February it is a Chinese New Year spectacular; in April, not surprisingly April in Paris, with a special French gourmet meal. The Oktoberfest is properly celebrated with stout German food, and at Christmas there is a traditional English holiday meal with baked oysters, ox-

The new building containing additional guest rooms.

tail soup, and a fine fat goose. This banquet is such a favorite that it is now served twice a year.

As popular today as when it first opened, the Captain Whidbey is an ideal inn for relaxing, soaking up a bit of island history, and enjoying the sparkling marine views.

THE CAPTAIN WHIDBEY, Rte. 1, Box 32, Coupeville, Wash. 98329; (206) 678-4097; John C. Stone, Innkeeper. A 25-room inn with restaurant on Whidbey Island. Open all year. Room rates from $28 to $60, double occupancy, with continental breakfast during the winter. Private and shared baths. Restaurant serves breakfast, lunch, and dinner throughout most of year; in winter, lunch and dinner only. Children welcome; pets allowed in cottages only, at slight additional charge. MasterCard and Visa credit cards accepted. Boating, fishing, bicycling, beachcombing, volleyball, horseshoes.

DIRECTIONS: Inn is at Penn Cove 3 miles northwest of Coupeville on Whidbey Is. From Seattle, drive north to Mukilteo, southwest of Everett, and take ferry to Clinton, then Rte. 525 to Coupeville. From Vancouver-Bellingham, take I-5 south to Burlington, then west on Rte. 20 to Whidbey Island via Deception Pass bridge. Continue south on Rte. 20 to Coupeville and Penn Cove.

Left. Stairway to the well-stocked library. OVERLEAF. The Chart Room bar, where business cards paper the ceiling and bottles are inscribed with names and dates. At right, the inn, outside and inside, showing its construction of madrona logs, also known as arbutus, which grows in abundance on the Northwest Coast.

PHOTOGRAPHED BY LILO RAYMOND

NASTY ANTIQUES JACK'S

LaConner LA CONNER COUNTRY INN WASHINGTON

A new inn in an old town

The approach to LaConner by car cuts across the flat rich farmland of the Skagit Valley, where red farmhouses, encircled by trees, sit isolated on the flat brown carpet of earth. In this expanse, with nothing to break the horizon, the sky looms vast.

LaConner itself seems like a miniature town. Most of its commercial buildings hug the waterfront; turn-of-the-century homes climb the hillside. LaConner's marinas are busy year-round with pleasure boats and commercial fishing boats that ply the protected waterway leading to the San Juan Islands. Most of the historic buildings have been restored to their original state or artfully modernized to accommodate today's tenants. But some buildings, like the combined hardware and marine supply store, are oblivious to sophisticated change, and their proprietors continue to do business in the deceptively efficient jumble that has always prevailed. It is a pleasing town, filled with intriguing shops, galleries, restaurants, and other points of interest.

The LaConner Country Inn is a handsome two-story board-and-batten building, built of cedar inside and out. The interior is trussed with massive beams and posts; light streams into the lobby through a large skylight. Just off the lobby is a comfortable, inviting library whose decor of cozy armchairs, fresh flowers, myriad books, and working fireplace suggests that it might have been transplanted from an English country house.

Guest rooms upstairs and down are pleasing and restful, and some open on a long hall leading to the pub and restaurant. The English-style pub is pleasantly intimate, with booths and a large room beyond the bar where guests must run a gauntlet of flying darts to reach the tables.

The restaurant is marine in decor; one dining room displays a beautiful model ship in a glass case. Brass lamps glow from cedar walls; silverware and glasses glisten in the light streaming through the mullioned windows that make up one wall. The menu is moderately priced and both varied and innovative. At lunch the chef might offer shrimp Louis along with a choice of fruit and cheese, soups, sandwiches, and goodies, such as mud pie (Jamaican almond fudge ice

The inn is built of wood inside and out to a design reminiscent of traditional English inns.

cream). Dinner offers quiches, fettucini, seafood and meat entrées, and a small but interesting selection of wines, beers, and mineral waters.

The LaConner Inn is a delightful stopping place, the hospitable centerpiece of a charming town.

LA CONNER COUNTRY INN, 2nd & Morris, LaConner, Wash. 98257; (206) 466-4261; Mr. & Mrs. Richard Thompson, Managers. English country-style inn in historic waterside town. Open all year. Twenty guest rooms with private baths. Rates $27 to $31 single; $31 to $35 double, including continental breakfast. Children under 12 no charge. Additional person in room $5. Write for group and conference rates. The Publican Restaurant, open to public, serves lunch and dinner. Children, pets welcome. Master-Card, American Express, Diners Club credit cards accepted. Game room with pool table; Bartlett collection of antique memorabilia at inn; Skagit County Historic Museum nearby; hiking, bicycling, exploring town, fishing, boating, tour boat trips.

DIRECTIONS: From Seattle, take I-5 to Conway or Mount Vernon; follow signs leading west to LaConner. Coming south from Canada, turn off at Anacortes (Rte. 20) signs, go west and watch for LaConner signs.

Left. The main street contains fascinating shops and, still operating, the original farmers' seed store.

An island inn where harmony reigns, the food is great, and the view superb

Louis Gittner is an expansive man, the sort of person you like immediately. The Outlook Inn has the same feeling, rather like coming home for Thanksgiving. This is what the people who formed the Louis Foundation twelve years ago had in mind before they started renovating the musty old building that had seen many incarnations since the 1800s.

In those years the raising of sheep and produce was second only to smuggling as a livelihood on Orcas Island. The inn was first a general store and jail, later a hostel to serve the fruit and stock buyers who called at Eastsound by boat. Alert to the needs of guests, the inn also served as a dance hall, pharmacy, and barbershop.

It has now been restored to its turn-of-the-century ambience. The guest rooms sport bright floral wallpaper, brass beds, marble-topped dressers, and period pictures. The sofas in the living room hug a large fireplace; tall candles flicker on the mantel. Someone is playing the piano. Fellow guests play cards or trade stories before strolling in to dinner.

The Foundation is based on a philosophy of service to one's fellow man—a necessary frame of mind for running a country inn. This philosophy and genuine concern for people is apparent throughout the inn, but it is at its strongest in dining room and kitchen. Louis is a superb chef who has imbued the Foundation members, who form a volunteer staff, with a sense of purpose and courtesy. In the kitchen the keynote is harmony. The food is delicious, tastefully prepared, and graciously served by cheerful waitresses in period dress. It proudly upholds the menu's claim: "The type of food you hear about but seldom taste, good old-fashioned home cooking." Translated, this means homemade soups, steaming fresh-baked bread, satisfying entrées, and, of course, apple pie.

Next morning as guests sip coffee, awaiting a very special omelet, they look out the expanse of windows etched with floral designs to the island and mountains in the distance, where the sun pushes colors across the sky. There is no doubt the outlook is good.

Left. John Biethan and Teresa Reser, who cook, attend guests and run the inn with other members of the Foundation. OVERLEAF. Two of the exuberantly decorated bedrooms and a marvellously sunlit passageway off the dining room. Following are two pages showing, left, the Chapel of Light, built by the members in an idyllic corner of the grounds and, right, a haunting early morning view from the inn.

OUTLOOK INN, Box 210, Eastsound, Orcas Is., Wash. 98245; (206) 376-2581; Starr Farish, Innkeeper. One of the oldest structures in the San Juan Islands, formerly a general store and jail. Nineteen rooms with shared baths; showers on each floor. Rates $18 to $23 single; $21 to $26 double; 3 persons $23 to $29; 4 persons $26 to $27. Rates do not include meals, but dining room seating 50 guests serves 3 home-style meals a day. Children welcome; pets by special arrangement. MasterCard and Visa credit cards accepted. Fishing, golf, beach, quaint shopping village, state park, mooring for yachtsmen.

DIRECTIONS: From Seattle, take I-5 to Burlington, then west on Rte. 20 to Anacortes turnoff. Ferries leave Anacortes daily for Orcas Is. From Orcas ferry landing, turn left and follow main road for 9 miles to Eastsound.

An island haven for yachting fans

The route across San Juan to the Hotel De Haro at Roche Harbor passes through a landscape as rich and varied as a Brueghel painting. Sheep graze in buff-colored fields; a horse sips from a lily pond shaded by a stand of tall pines; small boys, armed with sticks, enact a shoot-out; black and white Holsteins amble purposefully toward a weathered red barn. Then, seemingly in the middle of nowhere, just round a bend, appears the Hotel De Haro, its three-story false front locked in a struggle with all-embracing vines.

The hotel has the flavor of a museum, and in many ways it is. The story of Roche Harbor and the hotel is the story of one man, John S. McMillin, a Tacoma lawyer who bought the richest lime deposits in the area. The lime business flourished; a town grew up around the hotel, which was built on the original Hudson's Bay Company building; and wealth and prestige accrued to Mr. McMillin and family.

The hotel had twenty-two spacious and comfortable rooms in 1886 and still does today. They overlook a magnificent formal garden cleft by a vine-covered arbor that veils a cobblestone path leading to the marina. Roche Harbor, surrounded by many islands, is deep and well protected, a mecca for yachtsmen. The marina provides complete dockside services: provisioning store, laundry, rental boats, plus nearby swimming and tennis. The hotel offers two luxuries cherished by sailors: a bed that does not move and full-length bathtubs.

A sportsman's paradise.

Anywhere there are yachtsmen, a good bar will be close by. The restaurant and bar are up the cobble path from the hotel in a Victorian mansion, once McMillin's home. Dining offers treats for the eye as well as the palate, with a view of the marina and distant islands. The menu prints tips on yachting flag etiquette: ". . . Service in the restaurant and bar will cease during colors." So enlightened, guests can turn to the food. The fish is particularly appealing: filets of red snapper over sautéed mushrooms, topped with sour cream and baked with mustard, herbs, cheese, and breadcrumbs; king crabmeat dipped in egg, sautéed in butter, lemon, pecans, and parsley; cod filets baked over spinach, topped with hollandaise.

There is time after dinner for a nightcap, then to bed and a gentle symphony of halyards slapping against masts.

HOTEL DE HARO, 4950 Rubin Memorial Dr., Roche Harbor, San Juan Island, Wash. 98250; (206) 378-2155; Neil J. Taite, Innkeeper. Large resort hotel, built in 1830, beautifully situated on harbor. Open all year. Twenty-two guest rooms with private and shared baths. Rates $32.40 to $38.40; suites $50.40 to $64.80. Rollaways for suites $6. Write for cottage and condominium rates and off-season discounts. Restaurant and bar in nearby Roche Harbor Inn overlooking marina. Excellent food, reasonably priced; good salad bar. Open to public for 3 meals a day. Children welcome; no pets. MasterCard, Visa credit cards accepted. Tennis, pool, boating, horseback riding, golf course in Friday Harbor, full-service yacht marina.

DIRECTIONS: Daily ferries from Anacortes, Wash., and Sidney, B.C., to Friday Harbor. From ferry landing, go through town to Roche Harbor Rd. Hotel at end.

Left. Hotel De Haro is the inn building for Roche Harbor Resort, a complex of many activities.

Homespun hospitality in a soothing island hotel

Seen from the air, the 172 islands making up the San Juan archipelago seem like shards of a broken pot, sifting the waters that flow into Puget Sound. The islands are formidable, densely forested, sometimes thrusting high out of the sea. The ferries that squeeze between them look too large to fit, or so it seems to passengers lining the rails staring at the mist-shrouded scenery.

First discovered by the Spanish, then explored by the British and Americans, the San Juan Islands have always held an air of mystery. After years of controversy, in 1846 the forty-ninth parallel became the line dividing British and American interests in the Oregon Territory. Because the San Juan Islands fell below the line, the question of ownership still rankled.

In 1859 an American farmer shot a pig running through his potato patch. The pig belonged to an Englishman. This indignity so exacerbated both sides that they stationed troops at either end of the island and girded for war. It was not until 1872 that Kaiser Wilhelm, of all people, arbitrated and the islands became American.

It is only a short walk from the ferry slip in Friday Harbor to the San Juan Hotel, still looking as it did in 1873 when it was a lumber company hotel. There is something friendly, even wholesome about it. It could be the handmade calico cats holding open the doors to the comfortably decorated, sun-drenched guest rooms. Or maybe it is just the soothing demeanor of innkeepers Norm and Joan Schwinge as they serve continental breakfast in the parlor, the only meal served. The parlor decor boasts a splendid harbor view and a nickel-plated stove with a rare mica door. In the interior courtyard the Schwinges have created a small gem of a garden, vibrant with old-fashioned flowers cascading down the gravel path to surround one of the island's oldest holly trees—with a real calico cat lazily scratching it.

The town shows signs of its proximity to Vancouver and Seattle, but this evidence of growth is attractive:

Cheerful but restful guest rooms.

interesting galleries, stores, and a variety of restaurants. There is plenty to do in San Juan, but there are few places as restfully inviting as the San Juan Hotel. It makes you want to go and buy a yard of books at one of the excellent local bookstores, return to your room overlooking the bright garden, and stay until they all are read.

Left. A restored bathroom, complete with a good old-fashioned chain-pull W.C. OVERLEAF. Two enjoyable highlights at the hotel are the delightful flower gardens and the adjacent shops containing a variety of unusual crafts.

SAN JUAN HOTEL, Box 776, 50 Spring St., Friday Harbor, Wash. 98250; (206) 378-2070; Norm and Joan Schwinge, Innkeepers. Quaint and restful hotel with views of water and flower-filled patio. Open all year. Ten guest rooms share 3 baths. Rates $23 single; $28 to $34 double; double and twin, 2 persons $36; 3 persons $40; extra guest $5. Complimentary continental breakfast. Good, inexpensive restaurants nearby. Children accepted but not encouraged; no pets. MasterCard, Visa credit cards accepted. Whale Museum, Marine Laboratories, historic sites, biking, fishing, boating, tennis courts, golf course. Interesting shops in town.

DIRECTIONS: Daily ferries from Anacortes, Wash., and Sidney, B.C., to Friday Harbor. San Juan Airlines has frequent service from Seattle. Hotel ½ block from ferry landing.

Indian Arm   # WIGWAM INN   **BRITISH COLUMBIA**

Luxurious living in the wilderness

Their secret way of preparing salmon is unique and unforgettable.

The motorboat idles past rows of yachts berthed in marinas at Deep Cove, then picks up speed. The mountains rise taller as we race up Indian Arm. The inn ahead looks small, but when we dock it comes into full view: a tall, weathered building with white porch rail and staircase—the type of "summer cottage" built by the wealthy at the turn of the century.

Building of the inn, planned as a showpiece of luxury and modernity for the rich and discriminating, was started in 1906. It failed for lack of funds and was completed by a colorful Prussian aristocrat, Alvo von Alvensleben, with a little help from his friend champagne heiress Emma Munn and, it was rumored, Kaiser Wilhelm. Alvo turned it into a German *Loftkurot,* or fresh air resort, and for years the air was redolent with the smell of beer and sausages. The war put an end to the party, and Alvo skipped to the U.S. to avoid internment.

For years the inn went downhill, ending up vandalized by hippies. When Steven Wong and his group of investors recently took it over, it was a wreck. Restoration was a long and costly task. "If only we had known," says Steven, smiling ruefully. But now it is done, with no effort or expense spared. The staircase rises from the dock to impressive doors carved in a Northwest Indian design by prisoners at the Matsqui detention center. On the right, upon entering, is a bar, and beyond lies a sunroom bright with white wicker furniture and floral cushions and draperies. To the left is a fireplace and deep couches, and the dining area. The upstairs guest rooms are decorated in a style compatible with the inn's age. All are heated, have private baths, and are furnished with a mix of antiques.

In the dining room Steven is revealed as a true hotelier and not the barrister his business card proclaims. Everything has his mark of quality, from the petit point upholstery on the chairs to the food—a wonderful blend of native, European, and Oriental cuisines. Outstanding are the chilled parsley prawns, barbecued smoked salmon, and crisp Tsimshian-style barbecued ribs. There is an excellent selection of primarily German wines, and the service is discreet and courteous.

WIGWAM INN, Indian Arm, B.C. Mailing address, #1001-805 West Broadway, Vancouver, B.C. V5Z 1K1; (604) 327-0116; Western Pacific Resorts, Owner. Turn-of-century inn on 155 acres with 6,400 ft. of waterfront and breathtaking vistas. Eighteen guest rooms; private baths. Summer rates $60 to $75; winter $45 to $60. Two restaurants and bar lounge, open to public serving 3 meals a day. Children welcome; no pets. MasterCard, Visa, American Express credit cards accepted. Fishing for salmon, herring hake, flounder, rock cod; crabbing; canoeing; duck hunting; hiking (½ mile to Spray of Pearls Falls).

DIRECTIONS: Accessible only by boat. Phone Vancouver for reservations (604) 687-9558. Scenic tour leaves from Harbor Ferries Terminal at foot of Denman St., Vancouver. Alternate pickup at Government Wharf, Deep Cove. Take Second Narrows Bridge to Deep Cove Rd., continue to Gallant Ave. Wharf at end of avenue. Inn 11 miles from Deep Cove.

Left. The restored inn, sitting serenely at the head of Indian Arm Inlet. OVERLEAF. The view South down the inlet changes constantly with the weather and the time of day, but is always impressive.

Reserve well ahead for this hotel's sole accommodation

Billed as Victoria's smallest hotel (it has only one suite), the Captain's Palace attracts patrons from all over the world, who come to enjoy the fine food served 365 days a year at breakfast, lunch, high tea, and dinner.

This magnificent mansion in the heart of the city overlooking the inner harbor was built in 1897 by W. J. Pendray, a prominent figure in the history of Victoria. Every detail, from the handpainted ceiling frescoes by European artists to the elaborate stained-glass windows, echoes the opulence of the period and has been faithfully restored and preserved by the host of the inn, Florence Prior and her late husband William.

The entry door opens into a wood-paneled foyer, where a glowing fire burns in the handpainted ceramic tile fireplace. In this cozy room guests may take a cocktail—possibly the house special, a "Tree Climber," a potent concoction of spirits whipped into a snowy confection and served in an enormous cut-glass goblet requiring two hands to lift.

Each dining room has its special charm, and all rooms display the owners' collections of priceless antiques. The menu is geared to British tastes: kippers for hearty breakfasters, beef bits in Yorkshire pudding shell for lunch, steak and kidney pie, and a range of seafoods for dinner. A selection of classic continental dishes is also offered.

The grounds of the inn offer amusing delights. Mr. Pendray was an ardent gardener who pruned his shrubs into animal shapes, including a bear that is three times larger-than-life size. His topiary art continues to intrigue young visitors.

Dining is the inn's main attraction.

The fortunate couple who has secured a reservation (well in advance) for the two-room suite upstairs, with private bath and balcony, may dine in their own parlor. An old-fashioned bell-pull summons an obliging maid garbed in mobcap and long pinafore.

Victoria has many sights for the visitor, including a new provincial museum nearby and the famed Butchart Gardens outside the city on the way to the ferries. Though the spirit of Queen Victoria seems to hover in this genteel city, reminders of its more gaudy past are still to be found.

Left. A beautifully restored building, correct in every Victorian detail. **OVERLEAF.** Recognized as a major cultural art form, Northwest coast Indian art is alive and well in this carving shed in Victoria, where gigantic totem poles are in various stages of completion.

THE CAPTAIN'S PALACE, 309 Belleville St., Victoria, B.C. V8V 1X2; (604) 388-9191; Mrs. William Prior, Owner; Mrs. Laurie Wood, Manager. Famed for its restaurant, open 365 days a year for breakfast, lunch, tea and dinner, the Captain's Palace has one luxurious 2-room suite with private bath and balcony. The $85 rate for 2 persons includes full breakfast and complimentary gift. Suite accommodates 4 persons; rollaway available. Stroll in whimsical garden; sightsee and shop in Victoria.

DIRECTIONS: In downtown Victoria, 3 blocks west of Empress Hotel.

OAK BAY BEACH HOTEL

Victoria **BRITISH COLUMBIA**

Tradition flourishes in this luxurious seaside hotel

Victoria boasts the most millionaires per capita in Canada, and more than one live in Oak Bay. Dotted with gardens, tea shops, and boutiques, this charming suburb of Victoria is reminiscent of an English village and a good place to buy British imports such as bone china and Scottish tweeds. The Oak Bay Beach Hotel is the city's only seaside hostelry and the only one in the world to host a killer whale!

In the late 1920s and early '30s the hotel catered primarily to wealthy, conservative guests, both residential and transient. Today the atmosphere is more freewheeling and the guests younger, including Miracle, an injured baby killer whale that convalesced in the hotel's saltwater pool until he was airlifted to nearby Sealand, Canada's largest oceanarium.

The three-story Tudor hotel was built on the ashes of an edifice that burned in 1930. But the hotel preserves past traditions; high tea is served in the lobby, patio, and gardens, and buttery crumpets are still popular. Local customers frequent the Snug, a discreet upstairs pub where the regulars keep their initialed mugs above the bar.

Each of the guest rooms and suites is handsomely decorated, and all share the magnificent view of the Strait of Haro, Discovery Island, the San Juan Islands, the Olympic Mountains, and Mount Baker, which peaks to 10,750 feet.

The menu at Oak Bay Beach is continental, specializing in superb beef and smorgasbord lunches. A fine selection of wines is available at reasonable prices. Christmas is a special time for feasting on a resplendent five-course dinner.

As the hotel brochure states: "Pomp and circumstance has given way to a friendly, relaxed atmosphere, but some customs do not die. In our rapidly changing society, standards must still be maintained." And they are at the Oak Bay Beach.

Each guest room is different—let the desk clerk decide for you.

Left. Opulence and elegance combine in this quiet sitting room on one of the upper floors.

OAK BAY BEACH HOTEL, 1175 Beach Dr., Victoria, B.C. V8S 2N2; (604) 598-4556; Bruce Walker, Owner; Jorgen Kierkegaard and Kevin Walker, Hosts. Magnificent Tudor-style hotel on the sea. Open all year. Forty-seven guest rooms with baths, showers, color cable TV, telephones, and complimentary morning coffee and newspaper. Rates $35 to $40 single; $40 to $80 double; suites $65 to $125. Bar and dining room open to public serving breakfast, lunch, high tea, and dinner. Lounge open noon to 7:30PM serves hearty sandwiches, Cornish pasties. Children welcome; no pets. MasterCard, Visa, and American Express credit cards accepted. Within walking distance of Oak Bay Recreation Center. Tennis, swimming, 18-hole golf course, fishing, boating, bicycling. Adjacent to Sealand oceanarium. Grand piano in hotel lobby. Music for Friday tea, some evenings.

DIRECTIONS: From downtown Victoria, either follow Marine Scenic Dr. or drive due east on Fort St. to Beach Dr. Hotel on water between Victoria Golf Club and Oak Bay Marina.

Recreation, family style, in a perfect lakeside resort-inn

"We avoid the outside world," says Innkeeper Ken Hole. "No newspapers, radios, or TVs in the rooms. Just a lot of books." Which is one reason for the popularity of this luxurious lakefront resort.

Shawnigan Lake boasts the widest possible variety of recreation, including freshwater swimming. The outside world is kept at bay by 300 acres called Sherwood Forest and by 600 feet of lake shore. The handsome, white clapboard inn with sky blue trim is an ideal vacation spot for families, and many guests are attracted by the special festivities and meals at Christmas and New Year's.

The inn's emphasis on privacy extends to the names of its dining room, the "Hideaway," and its lounge, the "Retreat," where dancing and live entertainment can be enjoyed in the evening.

SHAWNIGAN LAKE INN, 2665 Inn Rd., Box 40, Shawnigan Lake, B.C. V0R 2W0; (604) 743-2312, 743-5566; Ken G. Hole, Innkeeper. Sumptuous recreation and entertainment resort hotel on Vancouver Island. Formerly a country club, the inn has been completely modernized for the 1980s. Open all year. Thirty rooms, including 6 cabins, with 85% private, 15% shared, baths. Summer rates, without meals, $27 to $37 single; $32 to $42 double. Rates with meals $45 to $55 single; $68 to $80 double. Extra person in room $30. Children 12 and under $19.50. Winter rates $5 less per day. Write for special group rates. Restaurant, open to public, serves 3 meals a day. Menu features English specialties. No pets. MasterCard, Visa, and American Express credit cards accepted. Swimming in lake or indoor pool; jacuzzi and sauna. TV and library lounge; racquetball, volleyball, tennis, badminton, shuffleboard, horseshoes, 9-hole golf course and putting green; sailboats, rowboats, canoes; water skiing and sailing instruction; salmon fishing and Cowichan golf club nearby.

DIRECTIONS: From Victoria, take Trans-Canada Hwy. 1 north to Mill Bay; turn west on Shawnigan Lake Mill Bay Rd. to Renfrew Rd. Inn at west end of lake. From Vancouver, take ferry from Tsawwassen to Swartz Bay, go south to Brentwood Bay just off Hwy. 17A, take ferry to Mill Bay Rd., go north to Mill Bay.

Gabriola Island # SURF LODGE **BRITISH COLUMBIA**

The bounty of the sea at the doorstep of this rustic inn

The most accessible of the Gulf Islands, Gabriola has become a suburb of rapidly expanding Nanaimo. Civilization has brought changes, but much of the island's rough-hewn rusticity remains unspoiled.

Margaret and David Halliday bought Surf Lodge in 1975 to escape city stress, only to inherit island pressures. For guests, however, the ambience is undemanding. The inclination is to curl up in the lounge with a book. For the more energetic, there are sports galore. Intertidal beachcombers return to the lodge with assorted bounty to concoct feasts in the busy kitchen; and, if requested in advance, the cook will prepare vegetarian meals.

Ample meals are served *en famille* by Rita, an outgoing English lass who calls guests "Luv" and makes them feel at home.

The Hallidays suggest rooms at the rear of the lodge for light sleepers—the popular bar hums into the wee hours!

SURF LODGE, Gabriola Island, B.C. V0R 1X0; (604) 247-9231; David and Margaret Halliday, Innkeepers. There is no finer vista of the Straits of Georgia than from the many-windowed Surf Lodge. Stone fireplaces in rustic main lounge and adjoining Compass Room lend warmth. Open from May 1 to end of Sept. Twenty rooms in lodge and 9 cottages. Rates with meals $45 to $49 single; $72 to $77 double. Without meals, $27.50 single; $30 to $35 double. Dining room serves 3 meals a day, plus afternoon and evening tea and coffee. Open to public for lunch and dinner by reservation. Children over 4 welcome; no pets. MasterCard and Visa credit cards accepted. Swimming in ocean or pool, fishing, boating, tennis, table tennis, shuffleboard, horseshoes, badminton, archery, cycling, hiking; golf course nearby.

DIRECTIONS: From Victoria, take Island Hwy. north 70 miles to Nanaimo. From Vancouver, take ferry from Horseshoe Bay to Nanaimo. From Nanaimo, take Gabriola ferry. Guests will be met at ferry dock on request.

Galiano Island

GALIANO LODGE

BRITISH COLUMBIA

A whimsical inn on a paradisiacal island

A pleasant ferryboat ride from Vancouver, Victoria, or from the Gulf Islands, Galiano Island was settled by loggers and fishermen. Now it is the choice of artists, professionals, retired executives, and many others as one of earth's very special places to live. Rozanne Shuey and Sonja Maans, who bought Galiano Lodge in 1976, agree.

Rozanne, who spent twenty years in the hotel business, recalls: "We inherited problems from waist-high weeds to disjointed screen doors. It had been through seven bankruptcies. We tied the place together, but we have tons of plans. It just keeps on happening." Both she and Sonja are inveterate collectors, who scout auctions and antique shops. Consequently, Galiano Lodge is a place to expect the unexpected—the decor is intriguingly eclectic, the staff endearingly eccentric. In the bar area guests will find an amusing English carnival "Love Machine," a Mexican chess set laid out on an antique chess table, and a Victorian chaise longue. Drinks may be served on an Irish sea chest or on a hand-carved Mexican coffee table and consumed to the music of a player piano. The bar, popular with locals, is a good place to learn about local spots of interest: Bluff Park, whose cliffs rise 320 feet above Active Pass where the ferries come and go; Bellhouse Park, with acres of forest and meadowland; and Montague Harbour, one of the finest yacht anchorages in British Columbia.

Roses bloom in December in the Gulf Islands' subtropical climate.

The carpeted guest rooms are decorated with antiques and old country furnishings—tapestry-upholstered chairs, desks, bedsteads, and marble washstands—accented by bright bouquets from the garden. Only the picture windows and the conveniences bow to the modern.

Three seaview dining rooms, with pot-bellied stoves, oak swivel chairs, and matching quilted lampshades and tablemats, offer an excellent menu. Perhaps fresh blueberry hotcakes for breakfast, crisp fish and chips for lunch, and ribs marinated in a zesty sauce for dinner, followed by buttermilk pie, a favorite.

Next morning, for guests who set out to explore the island's glories, the chef will pack a picnic lunch complete with wine and checkered tablecloth.

Left. Above, a Viking sailing boat reproduced by an island craftsman. Below, the sun-drenched lounge and dining room.

GALIANO LODGE, Sturdies Bay, Galiano Is., B.C. V0N 1P0; (604) 539-2233; Rozanne Shuey and Sonja Maans, Owners; Reg and Betty Edwards, Innkeepers. An island lodge with unsurpassed sea and mountain views. Open all year. Four units in lodge; 12 cabin units on waterfront, all with private baths and showers. Rates $34 to $38 single; $38 to $44 double, not including meals. Write for special rates for escape weekends for senior citizens, seminar groups, and others. Dining rooms serving 3 meals a day open to public 8AM to 10PM. Bar open until midnight. Children welcome; pets by arrangement with innkeepers. MasterCard, Visa, and American Express credit cards accepted. Swimming in outdoor pool or at Shell Beach or Pebble Beach (white sand, turquoise waters), tennis court, sauna, car and bike rental, 9-hole golf course nearby.

DIRECTIONS: Ferry from Tsawwassen (Vancouver terminal) to Sturdies Bay, 300 yds. from lodge; ferry from Swartz Bay (Victoria terminal) to Montague Harbour, 5 miles from lodge; courtesy car pickup. By air, 30 minutes from Vancouver or Victoria to lodge dock. Write for ferry schedules.

MAÑANA LODGE

Ladysmith **BRITISH COLUMBIA**

An oasis of fine food at dockside

Long a refuge for local sailors in need of rest and re-fueling, this unexpected oasis in Ladysmith Harbour has become a haven for lovers of haute cuisine. Word of mouth has brought diners from such faraway shores as Japan, Hawaii, and Denmark, and most have penned their raves in the guest log.

Overlooking a covey of sailboats nestled in for the night, the windows of the panoramic dining room admit the setting sun to be reflected in sparkling glasses on red tablecloths. The tables' ceramic candle holders, salt and pepper shakers, creamers, sugar bowls, and planters come from the pottery of Ruth Porter in Nanaimo.

Jeannette, a chic professional, takes your order from the varied continental menu. She doubles as sommelier, recommending reasonably priced wines in a charming accent. Following a crisp salad tossed at the table with the tangy house dressing—"a secret recipe"—she suggests oysters Florentine, plump morsels bedded in spinach and bathed in a rosy sauce Choron. For dessert, perhaps a euphoric chocolate liqueur cake. Jeannette's performance concludes with Spanish coffee, a delectable concoction of coffee and liqueurs she assembles with expertise and presents with a flaming finish.

On summer Sundays a champagne breakfast is traditional and features fresh fruit, homemade muffins, quiche, ham, oysters, sausage, and a dessert cart laden with cakes. With flowing glasses of champagne or cups of coffee, guests make their leisurely way to tables on the lawn or patio overlooking the water, while children play on swings in the back meadow.

Everything about this small immaculate lodge, including the five guest rooms, is done with care. "This is our home. And we want our guests to feel at home here too," says Thelma Stickle, who with her husband, George, and close friends Rena and Jim Mazurenko pulled up stakes in Edmonton, left secure jobs, and bought the lodge in 1973. "We had absolutely no experience at all. The first winter we played a lot of bridge." Now, after having made extensive

Left. The inn and the sea are inseparable with constantly changing views night and day, especially welcome while dining.

The marina from the flower-trimmed sun deck.

renovations and hired a chef and sous-chef, who cater to as many as 100 diners a night, says Thelma, "We're starting to hit our stride."

At Mañana, they run a tight ship. Those on board wish for no better tomorrow.

MAÑANA LODGE AND MARINA, 4760 Branton-Page Rd., Box 9, R.R. 1, Ladysmith, Vancouver Island, B.C. V0R 2E0; (604) 245-2312; George and Thelma Stickle; Jim and Rena Mazurenko, Hosts. Two-story board-and-batten lodge on secluded bay, with full-service marina and dining room noted for haute cuisine. Open all year except Jan. Five guest rooms, 4 share shower; toilet and sink; 1 room with toilet and sink only. Rates per room, $20 to $25, not including meals. No TV or radio. Children welcome; no pets. MasterCard and Visa credit cards accepted. Warm tidal water swimming, horseshoes, hiking, play area for children. Gift shop sells local pottery, jewelry, sweaters, and mittens made by Cowichan Indians.

DIRECTIONS: From Victoria, take Island Hwy. north 50 miles. Turn off 2½ miles north of Ladysmith, look for signs to lodge. From Vancouver, Horseshoe Bay to Departure Bay (Nanaimo). Go 12 miles south on Island Hwy. Watch for lodge signs.

Ladysmith # YELLOW POINT LODGE **BRITISH COLUMBIA**

On the doorstep to paradise

In the forty years since the main lodge was completed, Yellow Point has seen guests return year after year. They are attracted by the lodge's easy hospitality, its close bond with the natural surroundings, its mile of unspoiled waterfront, and ninety acres of parkland shared only with copious wildlife.

The realization of one man's dream and determination, the lodge was hand constructed by Gerry Hill, the eighty-eight-year-old owner; he built it in four years, rigging his own sawmill, finding water, and forging roads without motor power. It was, and is, a unique labor of love. "I look upon myself as a custodian," says Gerry. "Nature's the finest designer. I don't meddle with her." The lodge is much admired for its architecture, log work, and stonemasonry as well as for its spectacular site overlooking a vast seascape with snowcapped mountains in the distance.

The centerpiece of the lodge is the spacious lounge with views of the water on two sides, a vaulted log and cedar-plank ceiling, an arbutus tree (that Gerry could not bear to fell) rising through the floor, and a massive stone fireplace. Gerry spins tales, spooky and otherwise, to fascinated fireside gatherings. Ask him about the skeleton in the chimney, Alma's skull, and Brother Twelve. Or about his playmates, the killer whales, and Beverly, his pet faun, prone to leap on the campstyle dining tables. "I was the best doe on the island," claims Gerry, who has nurtured hundreds of strays.

Accommodations are many and varied, from large and small rooms in the lodge to three cottages containing from one to five bedrooms. Three hearty meals are served daily to inn guests, and there is mid-morning coffee and afternoon and evening tea with home-baked tarts and cakes.

A walk around the grounds reveals some surprises: a 200-foot saltwater swimming pool, hot showers in a thicket overlooking the sea, a steaming hot tub hidden in a copse, and secluded coves and beaches.

To stay at Yellow Point Lodge is to share the warmth, relaxation, and hospitality of a great country house party with fellow guests from far and near.

Gerry Hill with his labrador and several west coast potters.

YELLOW POINT LODGE, R.R. 3, Ladysmith, Vancouver Island, B.C. V0R, 2E0; (604) 245-7422; Gerry Hill, Owner; Ron Friend, Innkeeper. A handsome hand-crafted log lodge on the Strait of Georgia, popular for 40 years. Open all year. Lodge rates: room with bath $60 single, $47 double; with shower $50 single, $47 double; with basin only $45 single, $34 double. Cottages and cabins from $37 to $60 single, $32 to $47 double, depending on facilities. Rates include 3 meals a day served family style to lodge guests only. Write for descriptive brochure with special and group rates. Children over 16 welcome; no pets. No credit cards. Tennis, swimming, fishing, sailing, canoeing, rowboating, jogging and walking trails, volleyball, badminton, ping pong, horseshoes, dancing. Write for information on ski weekends. For more sophisticated dining, guests might try the continental gourmet menu at Inn of the Sea, 3600 Yellow Pt. Rd., next door to the lodge.

DIRECTIONS: From Nanaimo, go south 3 miles on Island Hwy., left on Cedar Rd. 2 miles to Nanaimo River, right on Cedar Rd. 3 miles to Yellow Pt. Rd., left 7 miles. From Victoria, go north on Island Hwy. 3 miles past Ladysmith, right on Cedar Rd. 2 miles to Yellow Pt. Rd., right again 4 miles. Write for ferry schedules from mainland.

Left. Despite the inn's massive log construction, the interior is warm and intimate. **OVERLEAF.** The inn sits on a great granite rock overlooking the sea and the afternoon sun.

Hornby Island SEA BREEZE LODGE **BRITISH COLUMBIA**

An island hideaway close to nature

The four square miles of this tiny island are alive with creativity, both man's and nature's. Potters, artists, sculptors, weavers of cloth and poems, and builders of houses and musical instruments abide here in harmony with the land, the sea, and one another. Visitors receive a warm welcome at the island's unpretentious hostelry.

"There are very few months of the year when anyone would prefer Hawaii to Hornby," affirm innkeepers Brian and Gail Bishop, whose loyalty to their balmy climate is well deserved. Warm seas and soothing breezes caress the shore at the foot of their cedar-plank lodge, perched on a bluff, where urban cares are sloughed off. In the distance Mount Geoffrey rises above the majestic British Columbia coast, an endless expanse of rugged rock embroidered here and there with fir trees.

A stroll along the sea-sculpted shore reveals wondrous formations from deep caves to lacy fossils. For history buffs there are Indian petroglyphs. Rock hounds may spot agate, basalt, concretion, garnet, jasper, and other gems. Eagles, hummingbirds, osprey, pygmy owls, finches, and woodpeckers flirt with bird-watchers. Meadows are ablaze with Indian paintbrush, columbine, dogtooth violet, trillium, shooting star, and forget-me-not.

In the lodge, guests mingle with island artisans in the cozy living-dining room, sipping aperitifs around the fireplace built from local fossils, shells, and rocks by the Bishops and their three sons. Brian is a fine

The hospitable innkeepers.

host and raconteur whose enthusiasm for conservation spills over into excited talk with his guests.

Gail is a splendid cook, creating salads from the garden, pies from the orchard, and entrées emphasizing fish caught a line's throw away. The long oak tables are graced with local pottery as well as with Gail's homemade breads and chutneys. "I just toss things together," she modestly disclaims, but guests have been tugging her capable sleeves for years urging her to write a cookbook.

Summer lunches on the patio often start with chanterelles, plucked nearby and sautéed, followed by buckets of steamed clams with drawn butter. Clams, mussels, scallops, oysters, and shrimp are hand harvested, and the Bishops' youngest son dives for abalone when the tide is right.

Guests feel very much at home at this modest inn and are likely to be sent on their reluctant way with small bundles of cakes as a farewell gesture.

SEA BREEZE LODGE, Hornby Island, B.C. V0R 120; (604) 335-2321; Brian and Gail Bishop, Innkeepers. Intimate rustic lodge on a tiny island noted for natural beauty. Open April 1 to Oct. 1. Ten cottages. Double rates, with plumbing, $42 per person per day; weekly $280. Without plumbing, single or double, $36 per person per day; weekly $240. Single $52 per day, $350 weekly. Children 12 and under $18.50 per day, $120 weekly; 13 to 16, $26 per day, $170 weekly. All rates include 3 meals a day. Dining room open to public for dinner by reservation. Housekeeping cottages available Oct. 1 to April 1. Co-op store nearby. Pets accepted. No credit cards. Swimming, tennis, boating, fishing, bird-watching, beachcombing, fossil hunting, ping pong, ponies for children.

DIRECTIONS: Ferries to Vancouver Is. leave from Horseshoe Bay for Nanaimo and from Powell River for Comox, then from Buckley Bay to Denman Is. and on to Hornby. Ferries leave Buckley Bay on the hour for Hornby Is. up to 6PM daily, except Friday, when last run is 10PM.

The main lodge, where conviviality reigns.

Left. No where on the island is ever far from the beach, with its exhilarating sea air.

Qualicum Beach # QUALICUM COLLEGE INN **BRITISH COLUMBIA**

Medieval in theme, modern in comfort

This beautiful red-roofed Tudor-style building has been transformed from a spartan boys' school into a luxurious hotel, centerpiece of a justly famed resort area.

Today's guests are pampered with breakfast in bed or sent off for an outing with picnic basket in hand to explore the surrounding scenic splendors.

Only a few trophies remain from former school days, but the medieval Old Boys Dining Hall is now the inn's restaurant, serving fine food prepared by the master hand of a Scottish chef and on occasion featuring a full medieval feast.

The inn has its own 700-foot beach, and the area abounds in recreational delights. A visit to nearby Quinsam Hatchery, with its nature trails and picnic grounds, makes an enjoyable excursion, especially for the ardent salmon and steelhead fisherman.

QUALICUM COLLEGE INN, College Rd., Qualicum Beach, Vancouver Is., B.C. Box 99, Qualicum Beach, B.C. V0R 2T0; (604) 752-9262; Kerry Keilty, Manager. Luxurious accommodations and fine food in resort inn overlooking Straits of Georgia. Open all year. Fifty guest rooms with private baths. Twin room $38 in season; $32 off season; double room $32 and $28. Cots and cribs $5. Write for package rates. Fine restaurant, open to public, serves 3 meals a day. Children welcome; pets accepted. MasterCard, Visa credit cards accepted. Jazz weekends with noted performers a specialty. Indoor swimming pool, sauna, whirlpool, private beach; nearby riding, golf, fishing, hunting, skiing. Bicycling and nature trails.

DIRECTIONS: From Vancouver, take ferry from Horseshoe Bay to Nanaimo. Drive north 30 miles to Qualicum Beach. From Victoria, go north on Rte. 19.